THE MINNESOTA
WALK BOOK

Volume IV

THE MINNESOTA WALK BOOK

James W. Buchanan
illustrated by Michael Leonard

*A Guide to Hiking
and Cross-Country Skiing in the
Metroland Region of Minnesota*

Volume IV

NODIN PRESS

Minneapolis, Minnesota

ISBN 0-931714-03-6

Nodin Press, a division of Micawber's Inc., 519 North Third Street, Minneapolis, MN 55401.

Printed in U.S.A. at
Harrison Smith-Lund Press, Minneapolis.

This book is dedicated to all those who enjoy the natural beauties of Metroland.

About the Author

Jim Buchanan, a native of South Dakota, moved to Minnesota with his family while he was still in school. It was in Bemidji, while in his teens, that he became interested in the Minnesota woods.

He earned an A.S. degree from the North Dakota School of Forestry and also studied at the Michigan College of Mining and Technology at Houghton. Later, at Bemidji State College, he majored in the social and biological sciences and received a B.S. degree. Jim went on to earn a Master's Degree at the University of Minnesota at Duluth where he now resides with his family.

Jim Buchanan's education and work experiences have lead him to write about his first interest, the foot trails of Minnesota. In each of the six tourism regions of the state he has found unexpected treasures.

Table of Contents

FOREWORD

It was a sunny September day in 1977 that I had the pleasure of interviewing (during a hike, of course) Jim Buchanan, for a *St. Paul Pioneer Press* feature article.

Having read with great interest his *Minnesota Walk Book* Volumes I and II, I was eager to meet the man who had this knack of making me want to get out of my chair, put on my hiking boots and head down the nearest trail.

Like many people, before hiking with Buchanan I never would have believed that St. Paul and Minneapolis could be such a haven for the walker. This pathfinding wizard discovered some exceedingly beautiful walking areas in the Twin Cities, and he invited me to find some of these with him for our interview.

He asked me where I lived. I told him the East Side of St. Paul. He asked if there was a park nearby. I told him Battle Creek Park was right across the street. He asked if I had hiked through it. I told him that I was afraid not! So he suggested we check out that territory.

And with Jim Buchanan's help, I discovered I had some very scenic hiking trails right in my own backyard. Off we went through the park, up a trail also used for cross-country skiing, and on a hill we got a spectacular view of the Mississippi River and downtown St. Paul.

Buchanan kept talking into his tape recorder along the route. For example, he said, "Beautiful view of the city skyline up here . . . trails should be better marked . . . many 'informal' trails . . . unusual to have a park right in the middle of a residential area . . ."

He'd point out flowers and trees along the trail, say "Listen!" when he'd hear a warbler or a finch, and he'd tell me about some of the history he'd learned about the area before we hiked it. We walked at a moderate pace, obviously concerned with capturing the sights and sounds more than meeting some deadline. As one whose job it is to meet deadlines, I found the walk particularly relaxing, and I remember thinking to myself that I should slow down more often and take greater care to observe the beauty around me.

Buchanan was in the Twin Cities for several days to compile

information for ths "Metroland" volume, and during that time he called me several times at the office to tell me about this trail or that trail. He told me about the trails at Fort Snelling, for example, and Crosby Lake, and the Hennepin County Reserves. All were within a short distance of my home; yet I hadn't known about these trails. Buchanan was my source of information, and he was so enthusiastic about Twin Cities hiking that I could hardly keep myself sitting at my desk!

The great thing about Buchanan's writing is that your appetite for hiking gets whetted. You are presented with a picture of what's ahead down the trail and know what to expect when you arrive at the "trail starts here" sign.

Sylvia H. Lang

Introduction

The Minnesota Walk Book Volume IV, Metroland, is the fourth in a series of guide books to the foot trails of the six Minnesota Department of Economic Development tourism regions.

It is the aim of the Minnesota Walk Books to show that there are trails for hikers no matter where you live in Minnesota. You do not have to travel very far to find a wide range of hiking experiences. Each of the six Minnesota regions — Arrowhead, Heartland, Hiawathaland, Metroland, Pioneerland, and Vikingland offers some unique characteristics as well as some that are common to all regions.

Presently there are no backpacking trails in Metroland. However, this condition is subject to change. Parts of three Minnesota Department of Natural Resources corridor trails — Luce Line, Minnesota-Wisconsin Boundary Trail, and the Minnesota Valley Trails will be in Metroland. In time there may be facilities to allow these corridor trails to be used by backpackers; but now there are many areas which have campgrounds, picnic areas, nature centers, and other facilities.

Metroland: Geology, Vegetation, and Wildlife

When people hear the word Metroland, they generally think of St. Paul and Minneapolis. Metroland, however, is an eight county region made up of Anoka, Carver, Dakota, Hennepin, Ramsey, Scott, Washington, and Wright counties. The region has an area of 9,042 square kilometers (3,494 square miles) and a population of 1,913,545. This is 4% of the total area of Minnesota and 50% of its population. Metroland has large areas of forests, prairies, lakes and wetlands as well as cities, towns, and farms.

GEOLOGY

Metroland is in a large depression in Precambrian rock. This depression is named the Hollandale Embayment. It is shaped like a bowl. The deepest part is in the Twin Cities area. A series of seas covered what is now Minnesota. Deposits of sandstone and limestone from the seas filled the embayment. Four hundred fifty thousand years later glacial ice moved from the north and covered the region with a mile-high sheet of ice. In the process of coming and going, the glaciers pushed soil and rock into rolling hills called moraines. Lakes, ponds, and marshy places formed between the hills. When the glaciers melted, melt water formed large, temporary lakes which were drained by glacial rivers. The tremendous volumes of melt water flowing in these rivers poured through the drainage systems. The water cut through the glacial deposits into the sedimentary rock which seas had formed millions of years before. The resulting exposures of sandstone and limestone in valley-side bluffs form some of the most scenic places in Metroland.

Much of the limestone in Metroland has been removed by erosion. Because of this, Metroland does not have the limestone caves that are found in southeastern Minnesota. (See Minnesota Walk Book Volume III, Hiawathaland.) However, the sandstone under the limestone is deep enough for caves in certain areas. The best known sandstone caves are along the Minnesota and Mississippi Rivers in the Twin Cities. These include the famous Carver's Cave where Captain Jonathan Carver said he received in 1767 a deed from the Dakota Indians for a large tract of land in the present states of Minnesota and Wisconsin. Carver's Cave was known to the Dakota Indians as Wakon-teebe or Dwelling of the Great Spirit.

At the present time some of the sandstone caves are used for storage and the growing of mushrooms. One is even in use as a nightclub.

Since the departure of the last ice age, the vegetative cover of Metroland changed from lichen to tundra to taiga to pine forest to deciduous forest to prairie. Most of Metroland now favors the growth of hardwood trees. If it were not for the activities of modern man, most of the region probably would be covered by oak-type forests.

WILDLIFE

It is not within the scope of this book to attempt to list the many species of wildlife found in Metroland. There are excellent books which deal with the subject in detail and they will be noted in the suggested reading in the appendix.

While some of the large wildlife such as buffalo, elk, moose, bear, and wolf are no longer found living free and wild in Metroland, there are still many species of wildlife in the region. Even the inner-city parks of St. Paul and Minnesota have small mammals and many birds including waterfowl. Many people find it useful to carry a wildlife guide and to record their sightings while on the trails. Binoculars are worth their weight.

HUMAN HISTORY

From the end of the last ice age, about 10,000 years ago, and probably before, Metroland has been the home of many tribes of Native Americans. Archaeological digs have produced material dating from the time of pre-historic hunters as well as from tribes which had contact with the European explorers.

The last tribe to live in the Metroland Region was the Dakota. The name Dakota means "league" or "alliance". It is a term which implies friendship. Another name that some Dakotas favored was Oceti-Sakowin or the Seven Council Fires. Both of these names show that the Dakota was a nation of many allied peoples.

13

The name Sioux was given to the Dakota by their enemies. It is taken from an Algonquian word, Nadouesioux, which means Little Snakes, another way of saying "enemy".

The Dakota Indians occupied most of the land which became Minnesota. They were driven out of the northern part of their area by the Ojibway, and in the 1850's most of their remaining lands were signed away by treaty.

The first Europeans arrived in the late seventeenth century. They were French explorers. For many years the French traded in the region. After the fall of New France in 1763, Montreal-based fur trading companies moved into the area. They had control of the Indian trade even after Metroland became American territory. It was not until 1820 when Colonel Josiah Snelling built a fort on the Minnesota River that the United States controlled the area. The fort later bore his name. In 1853 the Dakota relinquished their control over the Metroland area in a treaty with the United States. Settlement started immediately, and it was not long before Metroland became an important agricultural and commercial center.

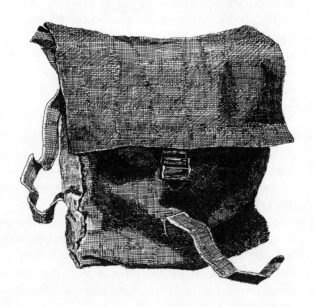

Hiking Tips

The outdoors belongs to everyone, and to avoid problems, remember the following points:

1. Consider the rights of other hikers. They have as much right to be there as you.
2. Avoid loud noises and horseplay on the trails. Wildlife frighten easily and you may miss your chance to see them. Besides, other hikers may be there for peace and quiet, and will resent noises which interfere with their enjoyment of the solitude.
3. Stay on marked trails to avoid becoming lost and/or doing damage to the environment.
4. Don't litter. Carry a bag for trash you may find on the trail.
5. Dogs can be a problem for both wildlife and hikers. Many areas prohibit them. Check the local regulations.
6. Unless you have written permission, stay off private property.
7. On most day hikes, it is not desirable to build fires. If you want warm food, carry it in insulated containers.

Personal Responsibilities:

Be prepared; have the proper footwear, clothing, and supplies. Match the footwear to the type of trail. While lug sole boots may be appropriate for rocky trails, they can be damaging to most Minnesota trails. Clothing should fit individual needs and the demands of the weather. Allow for changes in weather conditions. In Minnesota this means raingear, warm jackets, headgear, and gloves. Gear your supply load to the length of the trail, weather conditions, and the environment. Carry more food and water than you think you'll need.

Hiking Clothing, Equipment, and Supplies

Everything the hiker wears or carries should fit a need. Besides immediate needs a hiker should carry survival items that may not be used. Also, one must take responsibility to advise hiking companions of basic needs and emergency items.

Hiking gear should be of good quality. The hiking boots should be well fitted and well broken in. Two pairs of boot socks are usually more satisfactory than one. Long pants and long sleeved shirts are the best garments to wear on most hikes. A hat or cap protects the head from weather and insects.

For those who plan to be out any length of time, it is desirable to carry a day pack. Use a roomy one. Include food, liquids, additional clothing, maps, compass, matches, camera, binoculars, and first aid kit. Insect repellent, sun cream, and lip ointment should always be in the day pack. Even in the summertime hands can be exposed to wind and wet weather, and a pair of gloves can become a necessity.

Your chances of becoming lost while day hiking are small. Your best insurance against getting lost is to stay on marked, designated hiking trails.

Group Leadership Responsibilities:

When going on a group hike or any other outing, someone should assume group leadership responsibilities. Everyone should be informed of hiking schedules (time and place of departure and return), destination, travel arrangements, conditions to be expected while hiking, and gear and supplies needed for the hike. Each hiker should be checked by the leader before departure to insure that they have the appropriate footwear and clothing. On the trail leadership duties include the taking of head counts periodically, checking with each hiker to see how each is faring, calling rest stops, knowing the trail, carrying the First Aid kit, and keeping the group on schedule. After the event, the group may wish to get together to discuss the hike. Slides could be shared and problems discussed. All this should be done in order to improve future outings.

Cross-country Skiing

Cross-country skiing is a winter trail activity that can be pursued in many of Metroland's recreation areas. Besides the hiking trails, the skier has access to snow covered lakes, wetlands and golf courses. In Metroland, cross-country skiing is affordable, available and fun. No one has to travel very far to have the use of a groomed trail. This winter trail sport makes many Metroland residents feel the snow season is much too short.

Metroland
Trails

Afton State Park

Trail Use: Hiking, Cross-country Skiing
Fee: Parking

Afton State Park is in the township of Afton. This new park is west of County Road 21 (Saint Croix Trail) about 4.8 kilometer (3 miles) south of the junction of the county road and Minnesota Highway 95. In the fall of 1978 this park is in the developmental stage. There are no entrance signs and the access roads are not in driving condition.

The park covers about a 4.8 kilometer (3 miles) stretch of Saint Croix River shoreline. The vegetation is hardwood forest. The terrain varies from floodplain to some rather steep hills. When completed this park will be 520 hectares (1,285 acres) in area. It is projected to have 9.6 kilometers (6 miles) of hiking trails.

For further information write or call:

Manager, Afton State Park
5500 Quadrant Avenue
Afton, MN 55001
(612) 436-5391

Check with the park manager for park maps.

Battle Creek County Park

Trail Use: Hiking, Cross-country Skiing
Fee: None

This 26 hectare (64 acre) St. Paul park is on the west side of Winthrop Street, one block south of Upper Afton Road. A parking lot is adjacent to the Battle Creek School.

Battle Creek Park is named for the 1842 Battle of Kaposia. An Ojibway war party moved through the ravines of this park on the way to raid the Dakota Indian Village of Kaposia which was on the other side of the Mississippi River. The area is now known as South St. Paul. The name Kaposia derives from the Dakota name "Kapozha" which means "swift of foot". This alludes to the villagers' skill in the demanding game of lacrosse which is a form of field hockey. Kaposia was the home village of the hereditary Dakota chiefs who were named Little Crow. The last Dakota chief of this line was the reluctant leader of the Sioux uprising of 1862.

The park is on a range of rolling hills. The forest is mainly an upland hardwood forest. In among the oak, maple, and basswood trees are some aspen, birch, and planted conifers.

TRAIL

The trail is a two-loop cross-country ski trail with a total length of 2.4 kilometers (1.5 miles). The trail starts uphill from the parking lot. Cross-country ski trail signs mark this trail. It is wide and fairly level. The trail is rated as an intermediate ski trail. It is a good hiking trail for families with small children.

The scenic high point of the trail is on the west loop. It is an overlook from which you can see the Mississippi River and part of the St. Paul skyline.

In addition to the designated cross-country ski trails, Battle Creek Park has many kilometers of informal trails. Some of these trails may be old Indian trails. The informal trails are not marked. Also, a lack of park boundary signs makes it difficult to know whether you are in or out of the park. However, this condition will be improved. In the next few years the park will be funded for trail development. When the trail work is completed, Battle Creek Park will have one of Metroland's most outstanding trail systems.

For further information write or call:

Ramsey County Parks and Recreation Department
2010 White Bear Avenue
Maplewood, MN 55109
(612) 770-1361

Baylor Municipal Park

Trail Use: Hiking, Cross-country Skiing
Fee: None

Baylor is a developing park of Young America. The park is 4.8 kilometers (3 miles) north of town on County Road 33. It is on the wooded shores of 93 hectare (230 acres) Eagle Lake.

At the present time the park is in the process of expansion, both in area and facilities. It now has a manager's residence, an office, and an excellent picnic area. Future plans call for a nature center, an agricultural museum, and a day camp.

TRAILS

The trail system of Baylor Municipal Park is now limited to 6.4 kilometers (4 miles) of cross-country ski trails. These are not marked for hiking. However, there are plans for an extensive network of hiking and nature trails to fit within the projected nature center.

In time Baylor Municipal Park will be an interesting park to visit.

For further information write or call:

Park Department
Young America, MN 55397
(612) 467-3145

Blackhawk Municipal Park

Trail Use: Hiking, Cross-country Skiing
Fee: None

Blackhawk Park is in the Eagan city park system. The park is about 8 kilometers (5 miles) south of the Mendota Bridge. The entrance is not easy to find because it is unmarked. It is a block east of the Riverton Road, 1.4 kilometers (.9 mile) north of the junction of the Riverton Road and County State Aid Road 30. The entrance to the park is in a highly developed residential area. Very limited street-side parking is available at the park entrance.

23

The park is named after Blackhawk Lake which is a 15 hectare (39 acres) lake among the park's hills. Most of the park is prairie, but there is a band of trees around the lake.

TRAILS

The park has a 1.6 kilometer (1 mile) cross-country ski trail which starts at the entrance. There is a short length of black-topped path to a children's play area on top of the park's highest hill. From the play area the plainly marked ski trail winds around the hills which slope down to picturesque Blackhawk Lake.

This is a good trail for those not yet ready to hike in the deep woods, but it would also make a pleasant afternoon's hike for anyone.

For further information write or call:

Park Office
City Hall
Eagan, MN 55122 (612) 454-7802

Bunker Hills County Park

Trail Use: Hiking, Cross-country Skiing
Fee: Camping Fee

Bunker Hills County Park is part of the Anoka County Park Department. It is located on Minnesota Highway 242, about 8 kilometers (5 miles) east of the city of Anoka. It was named after Kendall Bunker who homesteaded here in the 1850's.

The park has group and family campgrounds, picnic areas, golf course, archery range, and conservation area.

Bunker Hills County Park is in the Anoka Sandplain. The Sandplain was formed over 10,000 years ago from drainage from Glacial Lake Grantsburg, a huge lake that once covered this part of Minnesota.

The sand hills of the park are covered by deciduous forest grassland. Several large plantations of spruce and pine have been planted in an effort to control wind erosion. Wind erosion can be a very serious problem with this type of soil. Geologists believe the basin of the 25 hectare (61 acres) Bunker Lake was created by a huge blowout many years before the first white settlers arrived.

TRAILS

There are 10 kilometers (6.2 miles) of trails which are used for hiking and cross-country skiing. The trails start at the Activity Center which also houses the offices of the Anoka County Parks Department. From the Center the trail bends around the southwest corner of Bunker Lake through a lowland hardwood forest. Part way around the lake there is a side trail to the north. This trail leads to a waterfowl observation dock on Bunker Lake. From this dock you may be able to see waterfowl and other birds that are attracted to the lake. Many birds stop here during the migration periods. It parallels the shoreline on higher, drier ground. Moving in a northerly direction, the trail passes a section of the park's picnic area. Shelters here are constructed of steel, concrete, and fiberglass.

After passing the picnic area, the trail turns west to the railroad tracks which are at the west boundary of the park. Heading south the trail parallels between the railroad tracks and the main park road for a distance before turning east near the golf course. After passing through another section of the picnic area, the trail returns around Bunker Lake to the starting point near the Activity Building.

On the Bunker Hills County Park trail the hiker passes through natural and planted forests as well as open grassland. This combination is one that supports high populations of wildlife. Walk quietly and be alert!

For further information write or call:

Anoka County Park Department
550 Bunker Lake Blvd.
Anoka, MN 55303
(612) 757-3920

Carl A. Johnson County Forest

Trail Use: Hiking, Cross-country Skiing
Fee: No charge

Carl A. Johnson County Forest is a unit of the Wright County Parks Department. The Forest is 11 kilometers (6.9 miles) north of Cokato on Wright County Road 3. At the Forest parking lot there is a small picnic area with tables, grills, hand water pumps, and toilets.

Like the other Wright County Forests, this 50 hectare (122 acres) forest is managed primarily as a wildlife area. The old growth hardwood forest provides a wide variety of nuts and berries for wildlife residents. A special effort has been made to provide a forest home for planted wild turkeys. Feeding stations for these birds have been set up throughout the area. If you are careful to make no sound, you may hear or even see one.

TRAIL

The main recreational development of Carl A. Johnson County Forest is a 2 kilometer (1.2 miles) trail, a wide, well-marked trail looping around the hills. There are some high places where one may view the wild woods and surrounding farms.

As a cross-country ski trail it is rated as intermediate to advanced.

For further information write or call:

Wright County Parks Department
Public Works Building
RFD 1, 97-B
Buffalo, MN 55313
(612) 339-6881 Ext. 182

Carlos Avery Wildlife Management Area

Trail Use: Hiking
Fee: None

This 9,310 hectare (23,000 acres) wildlife management area is mainly in northeastern Anoka County. The headquarters is about 8 kilometers (5 miles) west of Wyoming, Minnesota. Take County State Highway 22 west from Wyoming. Less than 1.6 kilometers (1 mile) from the town, County State Aid Highway 22 turns north. Continue going west. After 4 kilometers (2.5 miles) turn south. From this junction it is a little more than 3.2 kilometers (2 miles to the Carlos Avery Wildlife Management Area headquarters.

Wildlife management areas like Carlos Avery have two important functions. These are to provide hunters with public hunting ground as well as to set aside sanctuaries for wildlife where hunting is not allowed.

This wildlife management area has a public hunting area, two wildlife sanctuaries, a game farm, a tree nursery, and a research station.

Much of the wildlife management area is peat marsh covered by cattail and sedge. Around the wetlands are dry , sandy ridges on which aspen, birch, maple, oak, and brush grow.

Because of its low, wet terrain, waterfowl production and hunting are the main activities at Carlos Avery. It also has a growing deer herd as well as ruffed grouse, rabbits, and squirrels to draw area hunters. This area was one of three wildlife management areas that was opened to black powder hunting for deer. The area also provides habitat for non-game animals. Many fur bearers such as beaver, mink, muskrat, raccoon, and skunk live here.

The area has off-season use for recreational activities that include fishing, nature study, and photography. Many groups such as school classes and Scout units visit this wildlife management area. Group tours of Carlos Avery Wildlife Management Area can be arranged. Taking a guided tour would probably be the best way to become acquainted with this interesting place.

TRAILS

There are no designated hiking or nature trails in Carlos Avery Wildlife Management Area. There are, however, many kilometers of low-traffic roads which can be walked. When I visited the area, several groups of back-packing high school students were walking the roads in order to get in condition for a class trip to Isle Royale.

Throughout the marshes are numerous pools that serve as nesting places for many species of waterfowl. The road system of Carlos Avery allows the visitor to view and photograph wildlife.

For further information write or call:

Resident Manager
Carlos Avery Wildlife Management Area
Wyoming, MN 55092
(612) 464-2860

Carver Park Reserve

Trail Use: Hiking, Cross-country Skiing
Fee: Parking Daily $1.50, Yearly $8.00
    Camping Nightly $3.00

Carver Park Reserve is part of the Hennepin County Park Reserve District. This 1,429 hectare (3,530 acres) park is on the west side of Victoria. Turn north off Minnesota Highway 5 onto County Road 11. The entrance to the campground and the nature center is about 3 kilometers (1.9 miles) north of Minnesota Highway 5.

Carver Park Reserve has a nature center, a walk-in tent campground, a picnic area, and 22 kilometers (14 miles) of trails. There are ten lakes in the Park Reserve. Three of the lakes are fishing lakes with public access. These are: Lake Auburn, 144 hectares (356 acres); Lake Parley, 190 hectares (470 acres); Lake Steiger, 114 hectares (281 acres).

About a quarter of the Park Reserve is lakes or wetlands. Another quarter is woodlands, and the rest is former farmlands.

LOWERY NATURE CENTER

As with all nature centers in the Hennepin County Park Reserve District, Lowery Nature Center is an outdoor learning center. The Center conducts year-round nature programs for groups and the general public. For the casual visitor there are many interesting displays on a number of topics. The main building houses dining areas, classrooms, library, book shop, and a laboratory. There are also maps of the park reserve and the nature center. If you want to get more out of your visit, make your first stop at the Lowery Nature Center building.

TRAILS

Carver Park Reserve has 22 kilometers (14 miles) of trails. Some of these are self-guided nature trails that are part of the Lowery Nature Center. Others connect the Nature Center trails to the tent campground and picnic area.

The Lowery Nature Center trails are six self-guided trails. They are named Aspen, Cattail, Lake, Maple, Oak, and Tamarac. The trails range in length from .8 kilometers (.5 mile) to 3 kilometers (1.9 miles), and pass through woodlands, prairies, and wetlands. On some of the marsh areas there are wooden boardwalks that enable you to see swamp plants and animals at close range.

The Lowery Nature Center trails are wide and easy to walk for most visitors. Each trail is marked with an appropriate emblem. As an example, the Oak Trail is marked with a picture of an oak leaf.

The trail to the campground and picnic area branches off the Lowery Nature Center trails. It heads west and crosses County Road 11 just north of the entrance. At this point the trail angles to the northwest and then ties into a loop trail. This loop trail goes around Lake II and along the north shore of Lake III. It then goes along the east side of Parley Lake. The terrain of this part of the park is rolling open prairie hills with forest cover in the lower areas. Lake III is a 26 hectare (64 acres) lake. Some maps show it as Lunsten Lake. At the north point of Lake III there is a watch platform from which waterfowl can usually be seen.

The campground is at the northwest corner of the loop. It is on a hill next to Parley Lake—190 hectares (470 acres). There are both forest and prairie tent sites at this campground. It is a primitive campground with fire rings, picnic tables, water faucets, and chemical toilets. As in all walk-in campgrounds, all gear must be carried from the parking lot to the tent sites.

The picnic area trail is an interpretive nature trail that follows the hills on the eastern shore of Parley Lake to a picnic area on top of a hill. There is a great view of Parley Lake from this picnic area. Another trail goes a short way from the picnic area downhill to Cedar Point on Parley Lake. This trail ends at a secluded picnic site.

For further information write or call:

Carver Park Manager
Hennepin County Park Reserve District
Route 1, Box 32
Maple Plain, MN 55359
(612) 473-4693

Central Park-Nine Mile Creek Trail

Trail Use: Hiking and Cross-country Skiing
Fee: None

The parking lot for this Bloomington City trail is at the Moir Park picnic grounds at Morgan and 104th Streets. The picnic area is across Nine Mile Creek from the Bloomington Municipal Building.

When the first settlers moved into what is now Bloomington in the 1850's, they found a stream flowing through the area which was a tributary of the Minnesota River. The junction of the stream with the Minnesota River is nine miles from Fort Snelling. Because of this, the stream was named Nine Mile Creek. In prioneer days Nine Mile Creek was a source of drinking water as well as a place to fish. It is now a stocked trout stream, which continues to produce results for the angler.

CENTRAL PARK

Central Park is a long narrow part of 60 hectares (148 acres). It runs on both sides of Nine Mile Creek from east of the city hall to the Minnesota River Bottom. The principal vegetation of the park is oak.

TRAIL

The Nine Mile Creek Trail is a narrow 8 kilometer (5 miles) loop trail. It follows the creek ravine down to the Minnesota River Bottoms and returns back up the ravine to the starting point at the picnic area's parking lot. This is a well-marked trail. Along the way there are rest stops where you may relax on a park bench. On the bluffs 45 meters (150 feet) above the Minnesota River are scenic overlooks from which you can see the Minnesota River and the river bottom lakes.

In the winter the trail is used by cross-country skiers. However, some of the lower sections of the trail are very steep and should be skied only by those who have had considerable skiing experience.

At the Minnesota River Bottomlands the trail loops around an area of bottomland forest known as Welter's Wildwood Park.

Along the river bottoms are many kilometers of informal trails. These are along both sides of the river. In the future, parts of these trails may be in a designated trail system. Presently the use of these trails cannot be recommended.

For further information write or call:

Bloomington Park and Recreation Department
Bloomington, MN
(612) 881-5811 Ext. 230

Check with the Bloomington Park and Recreation Department for maps.

Collinwood Lake Park

Trail Use: Hiking
Fee: None

This new Wright County Park is located on the east side of 258 hectare (637 acres) Collinwood Lake. The park is 5 kilometers (3.1 miles) southwest of Cokato.

This park is growing as land is acquired. It may be several years before the final area of the park is known. In the meantime, with the aid of federal funds, construction of park facilities continues. Soon, Collinwood Park will have a modern campground, a picnic area, boat ramp, and swimming beach on the lake.

The park is situated among a range of rolling hills covered with a dense hardwood forest. Between some of the hills are low, marshy valleys. In the past these may have been bays of Collinwood Lake. In addition to woods and wetlands, there are open prairie-like fields that are former farm lands.

The mixture of land forms and vegetation found in Collinwood Lake Park allows the formation of good wildlife habitats. Parcels of wild land such as one found in this park often produce record white tail deer. Several huge bucks have been seen in or near the park.

TRAILS

As with the other facilities at the park, trail construction has just started. Presently there are about 2.4 kilometers (1.5 miles) of trail.

The trail is a well-marked, mowed path. Along the way there are hilltop views of Collinwood Lake.

For further information write or call:

Wright County Parks Department
Public Works Building, RFD 1, Box 97-B
Buffalo, MN 55313
(612) 339-6881 Ext. 182

Como Park

Trail Use: Hiking
Fee: None

Como Park is at Lexington and Como Parkway. It is 185 hectares (457 acres) in area, making it one of the largest in the Twin Cities.

Many activities are open to the public at Como Park. There is a golf course, picnic area, tennis court, swimming beach, and canoe rental. In addition there is a zoo, and an excellent conservatory where you can see species of plants from all over the world.

The park is named after 4.9 hectare (12 acres) Como Lake. This lake was first named Sandy Lake, but in 1858 it was renamed Como after the famous lake in the Italian Alps.

TRAILS

Como Park has about 5 kilometers (3 miles) of wide, paved paths. These paths circle the lake and go to various facilities. Part of these paths are the famous Como Park Tree Trek. This is a self-guided nature trail. Along the Trek are twenty specimens of exotic and native trees. These trees are marked with names and pertinent information. A Tree Trek Guide is available.

For further information write or call:

Como Park
St. Paul, MN 55103
(612) 298-4611

Crosby Lake Municipal Park

Trail Use: Hiking, Cross-country Skiing
Fee: None

There are two entrances to this park. One is at the intersection of Shepard and Elway Roads where only limited parking space is available on a side street. The other entrance is at Alton and Shepard Roads. This is a much better place to leave a vehicle because there is ample parking in an attractive, neat picnic area. The picnic area has a new building with a large fireplace that serves as a public shelter.

Crosby Lake Park is a 170 hectare (420 acres) recreation area in the wild Mississippi River bottomland. The park's forest is made up of oak, ash, maple, box elder, elm, and cottonwood. Among these native trees are scattered plantations of spruce and pine. Also, there are many berry bushes and wild flowers. Small, clear streams with fish connect the 11.4 hectare (26 acres) Crosby Lake with the Upper Pond. The wetland's in the park form several marshy clearings in the forest canopy.

TRAILS

There are about 5 kilometers (3 miles) of wide, blacktopped paths in the park. These loop through the woods and pass by ponds and marshes. There is a long section of boardwalk across an open water marsh. Upper Pond has an observation deck where ducks and muskrats are sometimes seen.

Connecting with the paved trails are other trails covered with wood chips or gravel. On the gravel trails one can see the tracks of wildlife. A wide, well-traveled side trail takes you to the banks of the Mississippi River. From the wooded shoreline, you can look across the river to Pike Island, a natural area of Fort Snelling State Park.

The trails of Crosby Lake Municipal Park are very popular with employees of nearby businesses. Many spend their lunch breaks walking the trails.

In the winter these trails are used for cross-country skiing.

For further information write or call:

Superintendent of Parks and Recreation
557 City Hall
St. Paul, MN 55102
(612) 298-4126

Hiking Along the Mississippi River

There is hiking along the Mississippi River near the heart of downtown St. Paul. Along the Mississippi River from U.S. Highway 61 to the High Bridge there are over 5 kilometers (3 miles) of paved sidewalk along the Warner-Shepard Road. The asphalt path is separated afrom the road by a guard rail.

As you walk along the Mississippi River trail, you have an excellent view of the many types of vessels that ply this important waterway. You may see huge barges and tugboats that look like waterborne freight trains.

On the High Bridge is a sidewalk from which you have a great view of the river and its wide valley.

Once across the High Bridge there are two interesting hiking places. One is Harriet Island Park. The park is .4 kilometers (.25 mile) north of the High Bridge. From Harriet Island Park you may board the river boats Jonathan Paddelford and Josiah Snelling for a sightseeing trip to Fort Snelling and back. A regular schedule is maintained during the summer months.

South of the High Bridge it is .4 kilometers (.25 mile) to Cherokee Heights Municipal Park. This 26 hectare (64 acres) park has about 3.2 kilometers (2 miles) of bluff-top hiking trails. From the woods you have an excellent view of the Mississippi River valley.

From Cherokee Park it is 2 kilometers (1.2 miles) along the Lower Mendota Road to Lilydale. Lilydale was an early day river bottom community of St. Paul. Because it is on a floodplain, it has been inundated many times. As a result, Ramsey County is now purchasing Lilydale where the county will develop a regional park. In the future, Lilydale Regional Park will have 6 kilometers (3.7 miles) of hiking trails.

Lilydale is across the Mississippi River from Crosby Lake Municipal Park. These two parks and Fort Snelling State Park will form three local parks on the Mississippi River floodplain. It is wise planning to use the floodplain for these parks. When park land is covered by flood waters there is usually little damage. At the same time, the floodplain performs its function of soaking up flood waters.

For further information write or call:

Superintendent of Parks and Recreation
557 City Hall
St. Paul, MN 55102
(612) 298-4126
Ramsey County Parks and Recreation Department
2010 White Bear Ave.
Maplewood, MN 55109 (612) 770-1361

Elm Creek Park Reserve

Trail Use: Hiking and Cross-country Skiing
Fee: Parking Fee:$1.50 Daily
$8.00 Yearly

Elm Creek Park Reserve is 27 kilometers (16.9 miles) northwest of Minneapolis on Minnesota Highway 152. After passing through the town of Osseo, turn north on County Road 121 (Fernbrook Avenue).

Elm Creek Park Reserve is the largest park reserve in the Hennepin County Park Reserve District. It has over 1,900 hectares (4,694 acres) of forest, open fields, wetlands, lakes, and streams.

Visitor facilities include Whitney H. Eastman Nature Center, a 1.6 hectare (4 acres) swimming pond, a large pinic area, and a playground.

At the Nature Center naturalists conduct environmental education programs for schools and other groups. There are also special weekend offerings to the general public. The nature center acts as a visitor center where you can become familiar to the features of the Elm Creek Park Reserve.

VEGETATION

There are 405 hectares (1,000 acres) of upland forest in Elm Creek Park Reserve. The trees include maple, oak, basswood, aspen, and birch. Lakes and wetlands cover 486 hectares (1,200 acres) which provides nesting opportunities for waterfowl. The remaining 1,050 hectares (2,594 acres) of the Park Reserve are formerly cultivated farm land now undergoing changes in vegetation by the long process of plant succession.

WILDLIFE

In spite of being close to a highly developed residential area, Elm Creek Park Reserve is the home of many wild creatures. Today this park is known for its large great blue heron colony. The birds have established a tree-top rookery in a large section of the park's forest.

TRAIL

At the present time the main hiking trail at Elm Creek Park Reserve is a 6.4 kilometer (4 miles) trail from the Nature Center to the picnic area at Mud Lake. After leaving the Nature Center building, the trail follows Elm Creek for one kilometer (.62 mile). The trail crosses the creek and over an area of hills. After crossing a road, the trail swings near the south end of Goose Lake, 25 hectares (62 acres). Like the other lakes in the Reserve, it is a shallow lake with a marshy shoreline. Lakes like this do not offer much outdoor recreation, but they are valuable resources to wildlife. Waterfowl and shore birds nest around the lakes. Deer, mink, raccoons, and beaver are attracted to the open water.

Beyond Goose Lake to the trail's end at Mud Lake (42 hectares, 102 acres), is a level trail through high grass and brush.

The Park Reserve's swimming facility is a 1.6 hectare (4 acre) sand bottom pond next to Mud Lake. The picnic area is on a hill overlooking the lake.

In addition to the designated hiking trail, Elm Creek Park Reserve has over 20 kilometers (12.5 miles) of cross-country ski trails. Much of the Park Reserve is wetland, and some of these ski trails may not be suitable as hiking trails. Check with the park's management as to the condition of the ski trails.

For further information write or call:

Elm Creek Park Reserve Manager
Hennepin County Park Reserve District
Route 1, Box 32
Maple Plain, MN 55359
(612) 473-4693

There is an Elm Creek Park Reserve brochure available from the Park Reserve District office.

Fort Snelling State Park

Trail Use: Hiking, Cross-country Skiing, Snowmobiling
Fee: Parking Fee

This 1,000 hectare (2,470 acres) state park is located at the confluence of the Minnesota and Mississippi Rivers, just south of St. Paul.

Fort Snelling State Park is unique. It combines a first class historical restoration with an outstanding natural area. The original Fort Snelling reservation was purchased by Lt. Zebulon M. Pike in 1805.

The mission of Fort Snelling was to establish United States control over the Upper Mississippi River. Later this role was expanded to keeping peace between the Dakota and Ojibway Indians and the encroaching white traders and settlers.

In 1819 troops of the Fifth United States Infantry under the command of Colonel Henry Leavenworth moved into the area and started work on the fort. After three years of alternately living in log cabins and tents, the troops were able to move into the fort in 1822. In 1825 its name was changed from Fort Saint Anthony to Fort Snelling. Colonel Snelling was in command of the fort during the erection of its permanent buildings. Fort Snelling served as a federal and state military post until it was decomissioned in 1946.

In the early 1960's the State of Minnesota started work to preserve part of the old military reservation as a state park. A major project is the restoration of Fort Snelling as it appeared in the first decade of its existence.

The restored fort is open to the public during regular hours from May to October. During this period, tours are conducted by guides dressed in costumes of the 1820's.

In addition to the restored fort, Fort Snelling State Park has a picnic area, a swimming beach, canoe rental, a remote pioneer group camp, a nature center, and a wildlife sanctuary.

Pike Island Nature Center has maps and other information that will aid in giving a greater understanding of the park. The staff at the Center conducts a year-round program in outdoor learning for schools and other groups as well as the general public.

The natural areas of Fort Snelling State Park are on the bottomlands of the Minnesota and Mississippi Rivers. On this flood plain are areas of forest and open grasslands.

TRAILS

There are three major trails in Fort Snelling. These are Pike Island Trail, Mendota Trail, and Wood Duck Trail.

PIKE ISLAND TRAIL

Pike Island Trail is a 5.6 kilometer (3.5 miles) nature trail around the outside of Pike Island. It is named after Lt. Zebulon M. Pike, a famous army officer and explorer. Several places in Minnesota and the western states bear his name. Among them are Pike's Peak in Colorado, Pike's Bay of Cass Lake, and Pike Creek near Little Falls in Charles A. Lindberg State Park.

The Pike Island trail starts behind the nature center building. There is a large sign with a map of the trail. The trail is wide, smooth, and well marked.

Pike Island is a flat land area. It is on the flood plain of both the Minnesota and Mississippi Rivers. Animal tracks in the soft trail bed reveal the presence of some wildlife residents. Among others, you may see tracks of deer, raccoon, fox, and beaver.

Elm and oak trees on the island are under attack by dutch elm disease and oak wilt. As a result there are many dead trees along this trail even though park crews are working to remove them. Some of the dead trees are covered with a blanket of vines which gives the forest a tropical appearance.

The waters of the Minnesota and Mississippi Rivers join at the northeast end of Pike Island. Here there is a short narrow point out into the water. After going around the island, the trail ends where it began, at the Pike Island Nature Center.

The second trail is the Mendota Trail. This is an 8 kilometer (5 miles) one-way trail along the east bank of the Minnesota River. The trail is across the Mendota Bridge from Old Fort Snelling. The Mendota Trail starts near the historic Henry H. Sibley home. In the past, this trail served as a pioneer wagon road and later as an early automobile road. Now, as a foot and snowmobile trail, it is an excellent way to travel through a wild river bottomland. This area is now a wildlife sanctuary.

The Mendota Trail is 16 kilometers (10 miles) round trip. Because of this, hikers must be prepared for a full day's hike on a wild trail. Make sure your day pack has enough food and drink. Do not underestimate your need for liquids on a long trail like this.

About 2.5 kilometers (1.5 miles) from the Sibley House there is a pioneer group camp. Scouts and other organizations may reserve this camp for their use.

In the winter the Mendota Trail is used by snowmobilers.

WOOD DUCK TRAIL

The Wood Duck Trail is located on the approach to a busy airport. This trail may be too noisy for some hikers. But, if you can put up with the sound of low-flying aircraft, there are some interesting things to be seen.

The Wood Duck Trail is a loop trail of 8 kilometers (5 miles). It starts and ends near Steamboat Landing. In 1823 the Virginia was the first powered riverboat to reach Fort Snelling. Now the Steamboat Landing serves two modern riverboats that carry sightseers from Harriet Island to this landing.

This trail follows the bottom of the river bluff and along the west shore of 48 hectare (110 acres) Snelling Lake. After passing Snelling Lake, the trail crosses the main park road near the park office. It then swings to the west bank of the Minnesota River. The trail returns between the river and the park road to the starting point. On the return the trail makes a loop around the island picnic area.

Being so close to roads for most of its length, the Wood Duck Trail cannot be considered to be a wild trail, but there are some interesting sandstone bluffs along the way. In addition, there is always something to see along a river's bank.

For further information write or call:

Park Manager
Fort Snelling State Park
2995 Sibley Memorial Park
St. Paul, MN 55121
(612) 727-1961

Riverboats Josiah Snelling and Jonathan Paddleford
River Excursions, Inc.
Harriet Island
St. Paul, MN 55107
(612) 222-0000

Ask for brochures and maps at the park office.

Girard Lake Park

Trail Use: Hiking, Cross-country Skiing
Fee: None

The entrance to this 25 hectare (62 acres) Bloomington municipal park is on 84th Street, one block east of France Avenue (Highway 17). In the center of the park's oak-covered hills is Lake Girard.
This 4 hectare (10 acres) lake has a marshy shoreline which attracts
many birds. These include waterfowl, shore birds, and wading
birds. Among the latter are cattle egrets. These are descendants of
birds that somehow made it to the New World from Africa.

TRAIL

Girard Lake Park Trail is a 1.6 kilometer (1 mile) loop trail around
Lake Girard. It is a well-marked trail that is easy to follow. Because it
is a level trail around a flat lake basin, it is rated as a beginner cross-
country ski trail. The north side of the park is landscaped, but the
rest of the park is quite wild.

For further information write or call:

Bloomington Parks and Recreation Department
2215 Old Shakopee Road
Bloomington, MN 55420
(612) 881-5811 Ext. 230

The Parks and Recreation Department has a map of the park.

Harry Larson Memorial County Forest

Trail Use: Hiking, Cross-country Skiing, Snowmobiling
Fee: None

The Harry Larson County Forest is on Wright County Road 111
about 4 kilometers (2.5 miles) south of its junction with Interstate
Highway 94. The Forest parking lot has picnic facilities.

Harry Larson Memorial County Forest is one of a number of
Wright County forests. As an area of rolling hills which is densely

forested, this is an area that has been kept in its natural state for many years. There are many wild forest plants growing here not common in the surrounding farm lands.

The forest is managed mainly as a wildlife area. An extra effort is being made here to attract and hold a flock of wild turkeys. If this project is successsful, you will be able to see those beautiful birds.

Harry Larson County Memorial Forest is now in a period of expansion. In the future there may be more trails in a larger park. At the present time there are 9.6 kilometers (6 miles) of cross-country ski trails and snowmobile trails. These trails are in loops that return to the same place from which they started.

For further information write or call:

Wright County Parks Department
Public Works Building
RFD 1, 97-B
Buffalo, MN 55313
(612) 339-6881

Check with the Wright County Parks Department for maps.

Hyland Lake Park Reserve

Trail Use: Hiking, Biking, Cross-country Skiing
Fee: Daily

Hyland Lake Park Reserve is a unit of the Hennepin County Park Reserve District. It is in Bloomington, south of Interstate Highway 494 on the Bush Lake Road.

The physical features of this 400 hectare (988 acres) park reserve range from marshlands to Mount Gilboa, the highest hill in Hennepin County. Mount Gilboa is 290 meters (950 feet) above sea level. From the top of this hill you can see the Twin Cities, many of the suburbs, and northern Dakota County.

For the visitor, Hyland Lake Park Reserve offers a number of activities. There is a picnic area, canoe rental, foot trails, and a day camp for groups. In the winter there is down-hill skiing on the slopes of Mount Gilboa and cross-country ski trails.

Richardson Nature Center occupies 80 hectares (198 acres) of the Reserve. In this section there are forests, grassland, and wetland. The Nature Center staff conducts a year-round environmental and outdoor recreational program. The Nature Center building has office space, classrooms, laboratories, and many interesting exhibits. The staff will furnish maps and other hand-out material as well as answer questions about the Reserve.

TRAILS

Hyland Lake Park Reserve has 9.6 kilometers (6 miles) of hiking trails. There are trails at the Nature Center, around Hyland Lake, and connecting trails.

There are three trails at the Nature Center with a total of 3 kilometers (1.9 miles). These are loop trails that start at the Nature Center building.

The Aspen Trail makes an elongated loop through an aspen woods. The aspen is called a pioneer tree because it often is the first tree to reforest an area after a fire or clear-cutting. It can't stand shade and soon dies out in the process of plant succession. Besides forest product uses, aspen is a valuable source of food for wildlife. The range of the beaver is determined by the availability of aspen. No aspen, no beaver. Other animals that are dependent on the aspen include grouse and snowshoe hares.

At the south bend of this trail there is a short path that branches off to a waterfowl watch site overlooking an open water marsh. It is a good place to see waterfowl and other wildlife.

The Oak Trail is east and uphill of the Aspen Trail. The oak is a tree that can grow in its own shade. This factor is a decided advantage and makes the oak a climax species in this area. Oak trees also provide an important source of wildlife food in the form of acorns. On the Oak Trail you may see trees that are affected by oak wilt, a disease of the root system. At the southwest corner of the loop there is a side trail to a boardwalk over a marsh. This is a good example of a waterfowl nesting area.

The Prairie Trail overlaps the northwest corner of the Oak Trail. The Prairie Trail is a grassland trail that is noted for the many varieties of wild flowers.

There are a number of small ponds along the Prairie Trail. Some of these have been dammed. This was done in order to protect waterfowl nesting sites from fluctuations in water level. Also, small islands have been built in these ponds. The islands provide additional protection from predators. Habitat improvement work like this has made Hyland Park Reserve a prime waterfowl reproduction area. Several waterforl watch platforms have been constructed along the Prairie Trail.

HYLAND LAKE TRAIL

Hyland Lake Trail is a 3.2 kilometer (2 miles) loop trail around the shoreline of 35 hectare (87 acres) Hyland Lake. The best place to start walking this trail is from the Hyland Lake picnic area. This is a well-marked, wide trail in good condition. Most of this trail goes through forest. At several places around the lake there are rest stops where you are able to sit and enjoy the view and the lake breezes.

Hyland Lake has a natural shoreline. Non-power canoes and cartop sailboats may be seen on this lake.

MIDDLE TRAIL

Middle Trail is a 3.4 kilometer (2.1 mile) loop trail that connects the Nature Center trails in the north of the Reserve with the Hyland Lake Trail in the south. Because this trail covers the central area of the Reserve, you have access to a wide range of land forms and vegetation that cannot be seen on the other two trails.

BIKE TRAILS

Hyland Lake Park Reserve has 8 kilometers (5 miles) of asphalt bike paths. The paths are in three connected loops of 1.6 kilometers (1 mile), 2.4 kilometers (1.5 mile), and 4 kilometers (2.5 miles). They are wide enough for two-way traffic. The grades of these paths are gentle enough to allow their use by bikers of all ages and bikes of all speeds. For safety, pedestrians and motor vehicles are prohibited from using the bike paths.

For further information write or call:

Hyland Park Reserve Manager
Hennepin County Park Reserve District
Route 1, Box 32
Maple Plain, MN 55359
(612) 473-4693

The Park Reserve District office has maps and other materials for this and other park reserves.

Jonathan Walking Tour

Trail Use: Walking
Fee: None

Jonathan is a new community of the town of Chaska. It is located on Minnesota Highway 41 about 32 kilometers (20 miles) southwest of Minneapolis.

Jonathan has been planned to provide for the needs of people, and at the same time, protect the natural environment. In this village it is possible to make a living within walking distance of your home. Jonathan has unique pedestrian transportation. A system of paved paths pass under the village streets so that you can walk anywhere in Jonathan without having to cross a street. Along the paths are rest stops and tot play lots.

For those who like to walk in the country there are trails to areas such as Henry McNight Park on Grace Lake and the von Hertzen Meadow. If you want to try a different kind of walking, visit Jonathan.

For further information write or call:

Jonathan Development Corporation
Jonathan Village Ctr.
Chaska, MN. 55318
(612) 448-2878

Lake Maria State Park

Trail Use: Hiking, Cross-country Skiing, Snowmobiling
Fee: Parking Fee

Lake Maria State Park is a 532 hectare (1314 acres) park on Wright County Road 11. The park is 12 kilometers (7.5 miles) west of Monticello.

The park is in a developmental stage and now has limited facilities. Plans are being made for its expansion. At the present time, Lake Maria State Park has a pioneer group camp, primitive family camping at the picnic area on Lake Maria, and canoe rental available. The lake is closed to motorized use. Lake Maria is a 73 hectare (180 acres) swamp with very little fishing potential. However, it is an interesting lake on which to paddle a canoe. There is usually some wildlife to be seen.

The topography of Lake Maria State Park is rolling hills covered with a dense forest of oak, elm, basswood, ironwood, aspen, and cedar. Among the hills are depressions, some of which contain lakes, ponds, and marshes. Most of these are too shallow for game fish, but they do provide for the needs of wildlife. According to wildlife managers, Lake Maria State Park has 205 species of birds, 23 mammels, and 10 reptiles and amphibians. Among some of the more notable birds are egret, loon, heron, eagle, woodpeckers, owls, and grouse.

Unlike many Minnesota state parks, Lake Maria State Park is without much human history. This is because no survey has been made for this purpose. Planned investigations may turn up some unexpected finds.

TRAILS

Lake Maria State Park has 14 kilometers (8.7 miles) of cross-country ski trails which are hiking trails when the snow is gone. The longest and most interesting is the 6.5 kilometer (4 miles) loop trail from the park office to isolated Bjorkland Lake. Because it is some distance from the developed section of the park, 11 hectare (27 acres) Bjorkland Lake is a fine place to look for wildlife that are drawn to its waters. Fisheries managers feel that this lake is the only one in the park that has much value for sports fishing.

For further information write or call:

Manager
Lake Maria State Park, Route 1
Monticello, MN 55362
(612) 878-2325

Lake Rebecca Park Reserve

Trail Use: Hiking, Cross-country Skiing
Fee: Parking Fee

Lake Rebecca Park Reserve is 925 hectares (2285 acres) in area. It is one of the largest parks in the Hennepin County Park Reserve District.

The park is located 4.8 kilometers (3 miles) north of Delano on County Road 50. Delano is about 12 kilometers (7.5 miles) west of Maple Plain.

The park's visitor facilities are on the shores of 117 hectare (290 acres) Lake Rebecca. These facilities are a picnic area, a swimming beach, and access landings from which to launch canoes and car-top sail boats.

Most of Lake Rebecca Park Reserve is former farm land. The farmers drained the wetlands and cleared portions of the forest. Since the establishment of the park, restoration of marshes has been the major wildlife program. The success of this program is shown in the large numbers of waterfowl and other wildlife living in the restored wetlands. The woodlands in the park have been enlarged by the planting of deciduous and coniferous trees. There are now over 200 hectares (494 acres) of forest in the Park Reserve.

TRAILS

Lake Rebecca Park Reserve has two hiking trails. One is the Deer Woods Trail which is a 2.4 kilometer (1.5 mile) loop trail around Lake Rebecca. On this trail you hike through a forest of basswood, maple, ironwood, aspen, birch, pine, and spruce. On the west side of Lake Rebecca there is a waterfowl watch station. From this station you have a clear view of the lake and the birds that live on its shores. The other trail is Marsh Trail. It is a 2.3 kilometer (1.4 mile) loop trail through an area of lowlands west of Lake Rebecca. The main feature of this trail is a restored marsh. A walk on this trail will show what can be done to improve wildlife habitat.

In addition to these two hiking trails there are several cross-country ski trails. Part of these ski trails may be too wet to hike. Check with the management as to their condition.

For further information write or call:

Lake Rebecca Park Reserve Manager
Route 1, Box 32
Maple Plain, MN 55359
(612) 473-4693

Lebanon Hills County Park

Trail Use: Hiking, Cross-country Skiing, Snowmobiling, Horse-back Riding
Fee: None

This Dakota County Park is 14 kilometers (8.8 miles) south of the Mendota Bridge. The main entrance is at the picnic area on Holland Lake which is on Dakota County Road 32 1.6 kilometers (1 mile) east of the junction of Dakota County Roads 32 and 31. The picnic area entrance is marked with a sign.

Lebanon Hills was formerly known as Holland-Jensen Park. This is a large park with over 648 hectares (1,600 acres) of rolling wooded hills, lakes, ponds, and marshes. Some of the named lakes in the park are: 14.5 hectare (36 acre) Holland Lake, 7.7 hectare (19 acre) McDonlough Lake, and 17 hectare (42 acre) O'Brien Lake. There are a number of unnamed lakes and ponds in the park.

TRAILS

To reach the trail system get on the trail around Holland Lake. Follow the trail to the right as you face the lake. This is a rough, narrow trail. About half way around the lake, the trail leaves the lake and heads uphill. On top of the hill you will see wide trails made up of old truck roads and new trail construction. These trails are not well marked nor are there any maps available of the park at the present time. However, plans are in the developing stage for this park. In the near future Lebanon Hills County Park will have 20 kilometers (12.5 miles) of hiking trails, 11 kilometers (6.9 miles) of snowmobile trails, 6.4 kilometers (4 miles) of cross-country ski trails, and 4.8 kilometers (3 miles) of bridle paths. When all the trail work is completed, Lebanon Hills County Park should have one of the finest trail systems in Metroland.

A short distance southwest of Lebanon Hills County Park is the Minnesota Zoological Gardens at Apple Valley. This zoo covers several hundred hectares and will have a trail system.

For further information write or call:

Director
Dakota County Park and Recreation Department
1560 Highway 55
Hastings, MN 55033
(612) 437-3191

Luce Line

Trail Use: Hiking, Cross-country Skiing, Snowmobiling, Horse-back Riding
Fee: None

The Luce Line is a Minnesota Department of Natural Resources Corridor trail. When completed, this trail will extend from Plymouth, a suburb of Minneapolis to the town of Gluek in Chippewa County. This is a distance of 166 kilometers (100 miles).

Like most DNR corridor trails, the Luce Line is built on an abandoned railroad right-of-way. When completed, it will have a main corridor trail and a parallel treadway. The main corridor trail will be used for hiking and biking during the summer months and snowmobiling during the winter. The parallel treadway will be used by horseback riders in the summer and cross-country skiers in the winter. Motorized use of the corridor trail is restricted to snowmobiles during the winter.

At the present time the Luce Line is under construction. It is not known how much of this corridor trail will be completed by the time this book is in print. At the present time the access points of this trail are at Vicksburg Lane in Plymouth and Stubbs Bay in Orono. As the Luce Line moves toward completion, more access points will be available to the public.

For further information write or call:

Trails Section
Parks and Recreation Division,
Minnesota Department of Natural Resources
Centennial Building
St. Paul, MN 55155

Manitou Lakes

Trail Use: Hiking, Cross-country Skiing
Fee: Parking Fee

Manitou Lakes is a 600 hectare (1,482 acres) recreational development that is under the management of the North West YMCA of Minneapolis. To get to Manitou Lakes take Minnesota Highway 25 south from Monticello for 2.4 kilometers (1.5 miles). Turn west on County Road 106 for 2.4 kilometers (1.5 miles) then turn north at the first crossroad. It is 1.2 kilometers (.8 mile) to the Manitou Lakes parking lot.

There are three campgrounds at Manitou Lakes. Two are for tent camping and the other is for both tents and trailers. Manitou Lakes has a separate picnic area. Two lakes, Bertram and Long, provide fishing and boating.

Manitou Lakes is made up of lakes, wetlands, hills, and plains. There are denser foests of native trees and planted conifers as well as open grassland.

TRAILS

There are 53 kilometers (33 miles) of cross-country ski trails in five loops. These can be used as hiking trails in the off-season. The trails loop around 55 hectare (137 acres) Bertram Lake and on the east shore of 65 hectare (160 acres) Long Lake. Being cross-country ski trails, the Manitou Lakes trails are wide and easy to follow. They are gererally in good hiking condition. Some of the hill trails are quite steep, but most are fairly level.

For further information write or call:

North West YMCA
4205 Winnetka Avenue North
Minneapolis, MN 55401

A trail map is available from the North West YMCA in Minneapolis and in Manitou Park.

Marsh Lake East Municipal Park

Trail Use: Hiking, Cross-country Skiing
Fee: None

The entrance to this 136 hectare (336 acres) Bloomington Park is at 98th Street and Abbott Avenue.

Marsh Lake is a low, marshy basin that is drained by Bloomington's historic Nine Mile Creek. This stream has its headwaters in a marsh in Hopkins. It enters Bloomington at its northwest corner and joins the Minnesota River at the southeast corner. Nine Mile Creek is about 24 kilometers (15 miles) long. During pioneer days it was a source of drinking water. The larger pools were used as swimming holes.

The park is in an area of hardwood forest around an open water marsh. The relatively undeveloped park is an exciting place to look for birds. Many species of waterfowl and shore birds are drawn to the ponds.

TRAILS

The development of the park is mainly in one designated hiking trail. This trail starts near the Bloomington Ice Gardens. and follows in a northerly direction the banks of Nine Mile Creek. While on this trail, one will see open marsh and grasslands as well as the oak-type forest that is characteristic of this part of Metroland. While on this trail, it is easy to forget how close one is to the center of the Twin Cities.

For further information write or call:

Bloomington Park and Recreation Department
Bloomington, MN 55420 (612) 881-5811 Ext. 230

Check the Park Department for maps and other information.

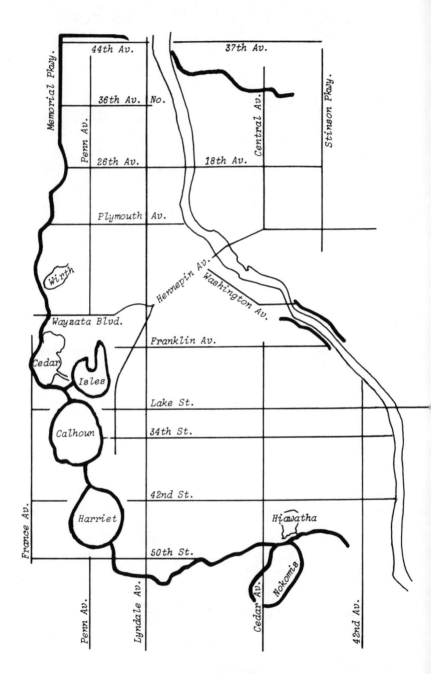

44th Av.

37th Av.

Memorial Pkwy.

36th Av. No.

Penn Av.

Central Av.

Stinson Pkwy.

26th Av.

18th Av.

Plymouth Av.

Wirth

Hennepin Av.

Washington Av.

Wayzata Blvd.

Cedar

Franklin Av.

Isles

Lake St.

Calhoun

34th St.

42nd St.

Harriet

Hiawatha

France Av.

50th St.

Penn Av.

Lyndale Av.

Cedar Av.

Nokomis

42nd Av.

Map for Minneapolis Park Paths

Minneapolis Park Paths

Trail Use: Hiking, Biking, Jogging, Cross-country Skiing
Fee: None

The Minneapolis Park and Recreation Board has developed a system of asphalt pedestrian and bicycle paths. There are over 50 kilometers (31 miles) of permanent asphalt paths as well as some kilometers of unpaved foot trails. The paved pedestrian and bike paths run parallel to each other along the parkways and are usually separated by several meters of space. Each path is about 2.4 meters (8 feet) wide which allows adequate space for two-way traffic.

The Minneapolis Park Paths go by a number of beautiful lakes. Starting at 42nd Avenue, you arrive first at Lake Nokomis. This is an 81 hectare (201 acres) lake. It was named after the grandmother of Hiawatha in Henry Longfellow's epic poem, "Song of Hiawatha"

In addition to the regular trails, there is a 4.3 kilometer (2.7 miles) exercise trail around Lake Nokomis. The Nokomis Fitness Trail starts at the north end of the lake. On the way around the lake there are 20 numbered stations describing specific gymnastic exercises to be performed. The fitness trail, an exercise system, was developed in Switzerland in 1968. This trail is the first of its kind in Minneapolis. Beyond Lake Nokomis the paths follow Minnehaha Parkway and Minnehaha Creek. At Fremont Avenue and 51st Street South, the paved paths turn north toward Lake Harriet (143 hectares, 353 acres) and circle the shoreline. The lake was named after Harriet Levenworth, the wife of Colonel Henry Levenworth who commanded the troops at Fort Snelling from 1819 to 1822. At one time this part of Minneapolis was part of the Fort Snelling Reservation. Lake Harriet is a family summer outdoor recreation site where families can enjoy outdoor band concerts while they picnic. Adjacent to Lake Harriet is the Lake Harriet Garden Center where you can see the beautiful rose gardens maintained by the Park Board. Across Rosemary Road is the Thomas Sadler Bird Sanctuary.

Directly north of Lake Harriet is Lake Calhoun. As at Lake Harriet, the paths follow the shoreline. The lake was named after John Calhoun who served as Vice President, Secretary of War and State, as well as Senator from South Carolina. The lake is 172 hectares (424 acres) in area. It is a popular spot for swimming, sailing, fishing and canoeing, as well as walking. Canoes are available for rent at the Lake Calhoun pavilion. It is possible to canoe from Lake Calhoun through Lake of the Isles to Cedar Lake.

Further to the north the parkway and paths circle Lake of the Isles, a 43 hectare (107 acres) body of water named after its two islands. This area is a beautiful place to walk where you can stop and feed the ducks year round. In the winter, it is a popular place for ice skating.

Northwest of the Lake of the Isles is 77 hectare (190 acres) Cedar Lake. The paths pass around the west shore of this lake. As at most of the city lakes, Cedar Lake is an enjoyable place to go canoeing as well as walking.

Beyond Cedar Lake is the Theodore Wirth Parkway and Park. There are several small lakes and ponds along the parkway. This area is especially favored by cross-country skiers. It has many kilometers of beginner, intermediate, and advanced ski trails.

Eloise Butler Wildflower Garden and Bird Sanctuary

This is a 5 hectare (13 acres) wild garden. It was established in 1907 and named after Eloise Butler, the garden's curator from 1911 to 1933. The garden is a place of rolling hills and wetlands. Most of it is covered by a mixed forest of needle and broadleaf trees, but there are also areas of open grasslands, bogs, and ponds. All through the garden you can find many varieties of wild flowers. Many specimens are signed with common and scientific names. A small rustic office houses a library and curator's office where visitors are welcome from 10:00 AM until 6:00 PM from April 1 through November 1.

West River Trail

There are foot paths on both sides of the Mississippi River from north of Fort Snelling State Park to just south of the Washington Avenue Bridge. The West River Trail is maintained by the Minneapolis Park and Recreation Board and the East River Trail is maintained by the St. Paul Park and Recreation Division. In the far past, these were travel corridors for primitive people. Now modern man uses these trails for recreation. The 5.4 kilometer (3.4 miles) blufftop trail is mainly a foot path. Only the section between Franklin Avenue and Riverside Park has a paved path for bikers.

Because most Minneapolis park paths are beside busy roads, they cannot be considered as wild trails. They are good places for urban dwellers to get exercise walking, jogging, or cross-country skiing. Many people get their first introduction to these activities on the park paths. There are many opportunities, especially near the lakes, to see wildlife. In the spring and fall many species of waterfowl, including Canadian Honkers, gather in park lakes.

For further information write or call:

Minneapolis Park and Recreation Board
250 South Fourth Street
Minneapolis, MN 55415
(612) 348-2243

Minnehaha Trail

Trail Use: Hiking
Fee: None

The Minnehaha Trail is an 8 kilometer (5 miles) trail from Fort Snelling State Park along the Mississippi River to Minnehaha Park. It is a wide, well-marked, easy-to-walk trail.

The trail starts at the Fort Snelling State Park steamboat landing. It passes under the impressive walls of restored Fort Snelling. Past the Fort there are some interesting exposures of limestone on the cliffs above the trail.

While most of the Minnehaha Trail is through forest, there are some open areas of grass and brush. After the Fort Snelling State Park boundary markers, the trail widens. Along the way there are wooden staircases that lead down to riverside trails. This is part of the Minneapolis Park system called the South Minnehaha Addition. It is a 274 meter (900 feet) stretch of virgin prairie and hardwood forest along the Mississippi River. It is a parcel of land that has never been in private ownership. In 1820 troops of the Fifth U. S.

Infantry had a tent camp here while they were constructing Fort Snelling. They were forced out of their cabins on the Minnesota River by the spring floods. The tent camp was named Camp Cold Water from the huge volumes of cold, clear water that flowed into the river from valley-side springs.

As you near Minnehaha Park, there is a turn in the trail to the right, passing a picnic shelter close to the banks of the Mississippi River. Soon after passing the junction of the Mississippi River and Minnehaha Creek, the trail enters Minnehaha Park. Inside the park there is a short walk on sidewalk before reaching Lower Glen. The Glen entrance has a large metal marker that gives some of its history. A foot trail leads down to a deep gorge. This gorge was cut out of deep layers of sedimentary rock by the tumbling waters of Minnehaha Falls as it eroded its way up Minnehaha Creek to its present location.

In the past, Lower Glen was used as a camping place by the Dakota Indians as they sought a sanctuary from their enemies, the Ojibway Indians. A few years later white settlers built and operated a mill pond in the Glen. During the depression years between 1929 and 1941, rock from the Glen was quarried for use in Twin Cities public works projects. Now Lower Glen is a park where visitors may walk through a stream-side forest. Along the trails in the Lower Glen are benches and picnic fire rings.

Near the edge of a golf course, there is a series of staircases leading up to the present loation of Minnehaha Falls. A short distance past the Falls, there is a statue of Minnehaha and Hiawatha. Minnehaha Falls was the inspiration for Longfellow's poem "Song of Hiawatha". Near the statue is the Minnehaha Park refectory where food and drink may be purchased.

For further information write or call:

Minneapolis Park and Recreation Board
250 South Fourth Street
Minneapolis, MN 55415
(612) 348-2243

Check for maps with the Parks and Recreation Board.

Minnesota River Valley Trails

Trail Use: Hiking, Cross-country Skiing, Snowmobiling
Fee: Parking

The Minnesota Department of Natural Resources is now constructing a corridor trail along the Minnesota River from Fort Snelling State Park to Mankato. This is a distance of 115 kilometers (71 miles). This trail is designated as a multiple-use recreation trail which means a snowmobile trail that can be used by horseback riders and hikers in the off season. Along with this linear trail there will be a series of cross-country ski loops of varying lengths.

At the present time, there are three trail areas in the Minnesota River Valley Corridor Trail that are open for public use. These are named Area A, Area B (Carver Rapids Wayside), and Lawrence Wayside. Area A is 4.8 kilometers (3 miles) southwest of Shakopee. Turn off U. S. Highway 169 onto Minnesota Highway 41. Just before a bridge crossing the Minnesota River, there is a dirt road to the east. This road leads to the Area A parking lot where there is a small picnic area with sanitary facilities. From the parking lot there are several short paths that lead to the main trail. This trail is a 13 kilometer (8 miles) loop trail on the natural levee of the Minnesota River. It returns to the starting point by way of a river-bottom lake shore. Because it is a snowmobile trail that avoids wetland, it is a good trail to hike.

Along the trail the vegetation is river-bottom hardwood forest. Some of the trees are very large. Because there is not much underbrush in this mature forest, you can see for long distances. This helps to improve opportunities for observing wildlife. Hunters report there are high populations of deer, rabbits, squirrels, and upland game birds along the river banks.

Area B (Carver Rapids Wayside) is .8 kilometer (.5 mile) west of Area A. The two areas are connected by a trail. Area B is owned by Northern States Power Company. It is managed by the Minnesota Department of Natural Resources as a trail area. Presently the parking lot of Area B is only open during the cross-country skiing and snowmobiling season. The rest of the year hikers are advised to park their vehicles in the Area A parking lot.

Area B is a tract of river bottomlands and bluffs. There are 9.6 kilometers (6 miles) of linear snowmobile trail along the river bank. On the bluff above the river there are 9.6 kilometers (6 miles) of cross-country ski trail loops. There are some scenic overlooks of the Minnesota River Vally from places on the ski trail.

Lawrence Wayside is the third open area in the Minnesota River Valley Corridor Trail. The Wayside is 8 kilometers (5 miles) south of the town of Jordon. Turn off U. S. Highway 169 onto Scott County Road 57.

Lawrence Wayside has park personnel residences, an office, and maintenance buildings. Visitor facilities include a picnic area and a rustic campground. This campground has both drive-in and walk-in campsites. To use the latter, the camper must carry his gear from a central parking lot to the tent site.

As with Area A, Lawrence Wayside is on a flat floodplain that is covered with deciduous forest. There are also grasslands in the area.

Lawrence Wayside has 17.6 kilometers (11 miles) of snowmobile trails. 14.4 kilometers (9 miles) of these trails are on the natural levee of the Minnesota River. The remainder is in a loop near the picnic area. Both sections of snowmobile trail start at the Snowmobile Trail Center across the creek from the picnic area. In the winter, the Snowmoble Trail Center has a warming house for use by snowmobilers.

Lawrence Wayside has 11 kilometers (9 miles) of cross-country ski trails in several loops that circle through the woods and by the river. The ski trail starts at the Ski Trail Center on County Road 57, a short distance northeast of the Wayside office. The Ski Trail Center also has a warming house. Both the snowmobile and cross-country ski trails may be hiked during the off-season.

When visiting the Wayside, it is a good idea to stop first at the office to check on trail conditions.

For further information write or call:

Parks and Recreation Division
Minnesota Department of Natural Resources
Centennial Building
St. Paul, MN 55155
(612) 296-4776

Minnesota Zoological Garden

This new facility is in the town of Apple Valley about 16 kilometers (16 miles) south of the Mendota Bridge. It is bounded on the east by Johnny Cake Ridge Road and on the west by Galaxie Road.

The developed portion of the zoo covers about 32 hectares (80 acres) of a 202 hectare (500 acres) area of rolling hills covered with woods, grasslands, and lakes. The zoo is home for over 250 species of wildlife from different regions of the world.

TRAILS

Projected plans for the early 1980's call for a 3.2 kilometer walkway around the developed section of the zoo. This walkway, which will be paralleled by a monorail system, will give the walking visitor access to facilities such as The Northern Trek, the Children's Zoo, the Minnesota Exhibit, the Tropical Rain Forest, the Aquarium, and the Education and Orientation Theater. When the walkways are completed, the Minnesota Zoo should have one of the most interesting and educational walks in the United States.

For further information write or call:

Minnesoata Zoological Garden
12101 Johnny Cake Ridge Road
Apple Valley, MN 55124
(612) 432-9000

Montissippi County Park

Trail Use: Hiking, Cross-country Skiing
Fee: None

This Wright County park is on the south bank of the Mississippi River in the west end of Monticello. The park has a modern picnic area and launch ramps for boats and canoes. There is a rustic camp for canoe travelers and some excellent places from which to cast for northern pike, walleyes, and panfish.

The forest of Montissippi County Park is mainly deciduous with some plantings of pine and spruce.

TRAIL

Montissippi County Park has 4.8 kilometers (3 miles) of hiking trail that is also used for cross-country skiing. The trail is in several connected loops. It starts at the picnic area where there is a large stationary trail map.

For further information write or call:

Wright County Parks Department
Public Works Building, RFD 1, Box 97-B
Buffalo, MN 55313
(612) 339-6881 Ext. 182

Morris T. Baker Park Reserve

Trail Use: Hiking, Cross-country Skiing
Fee: Parking

This 1,090 hectare (2,693 acres) park reserve is part of the Hennepin Park Reserve District. Morris T. Baker Park Reserve is adjacent to the town of Maple Plain on Hennepin County Road 19. The Hennepin County Park Reserve District offices are at Morris T. Baker Park Reserve. The visitor facilities include a rustic campground, picnic area, swimming beach, boat ramp, several day-camps, and a golf course. All of these facilities except the golf course are near the shores of Lake Independence. The rustic campground has 200 sites to accommodate tents, trailers, or mobile homes. Sites are available in wooded as well as open areas.

Hennepin County Park Reserve District was started at this park. In 1956, the Baker Family Foundation of Minneapolis donated 85 hectares (210 acres) of land near Lake Independence for use as a park. This was the beginning of a park system that now has seven major parks with a total area of over 8,500 hectares (21,000 acres).

Morris T. Baker Park Reserve is former farm land. About sixty percent was once crop and pasture land. Fifteen percent was farm woodlots made up of trees such as oak, hickory, maple, and basswood. The remaining twenty-five percent of the Park Reserve was wetlands and lakes.

There are four lakes in the Park Reserve. These are 324 hectare (800 acres) Lake Independence, 26 hectare (64 acres) Spurzem Lake, 12 hectare (30 acres) Halfmoon Lake, and a 4 hectare (10 acres) Lake Kattrina. The other three lakes are in the undeveloped section of the park.

TRAIL

Morris T. Baker Park Reserve has trails for hiking, cross-country skiing, horseback riding, and snowmobiling. The only hiking trail in the Reserve is Calling Loon Trail. It is a 2 kilometer (1.25 mile) loop trail that goes up and down hills through oak woods and grassland. The trail starts and ends at the Park Reserve District offices. The hiking trail cuts across the south end of a cross-country ski trail. This part of the ski trail can be hiked.

For further information write or call:

Morris T. Baker Park Reserve Manager
Hennepin County Park Reserve District
Route 1, Box 32
Maple Plain, MN 55359
(612) 473-4693

The Hennepin County Park Reserve District has maps and trail information.

Mounds Springs Park

Trail Use: Hiking
Fee: None

The entrance to this Bloomington Park is at the east end of 102nd Street. Mounds Springs Park is a 182 hectare (450 acres) tract of deciduous forest on a 45 meter (148 feet) bluff above the Minnesota River Valley.

The park is named after a site of 400 year-old Indian mounds. These mounds were in existence hundreds of years before the Dakota Indians arrived. They are part of our historical heritage, so treat them with respect.

TRAIL

The Mounds Springs Park Trail is a 4.8 kilometer (3 miles) self-guided nature trail. It is a wide loop trail with a wood chip surface. From the parking lot the trail circles in a clockwise direction. Along the way the trail passes a picnic area and several bluff-top scenic overlooks. These overlooks provide unusually good views of the Minnesota River Valley. You can see the river and the 577 hectare (1,425 acres) Long Meadow Lake as well as a forested river bottom.

In the near future, Mounds Springs Park Nature Trail may be connected to the Minnesota Valley Corridor Trail.

For further information write or call:

Bloomington Parks and Recreation Department
2215 Old Shakopee Road
Bloomington, MN 55420
(612) 881-5811 Ext. 230

The Parks and Recreation Department has a guide book of Mounds Springs Park.

Murphy's Landing

Trail Use: Hiking
Fee: Entrance fee

   Murphy's Landing is at the east end of Shakopee on Minnesota Highway 101. It is a historical restoration that features examples of the many different structures that stood here from 1840-1890, a time when Murphy's Landing was a pioneer Minnesota River settlement. Volunteer workers of the non-profit Minnesota Valley Restoration have moved many of these buildings to Murphy's Landing from many sites along the Minnesota River Valley. The restored buildings are strung out along a .8 kilometer (.5 mile) stretch of road. A visitor on the guided tour of the restoration will see Indian lodges, a trading post, a school house, Murphy's Inn, a railroad depot, a grist mill, several churches, a monastery, a gift shop, and many residences. New-old buildings are being added each year. At each stop, volunteers dressed in the attire of the period give a historical background of the building and answer visitors' questions. After visiting Murphy's Landing, one will have a greater understanding of pioneer life in the Minnesota River Valley.

TRAILS

There are about 6.4 kilometers (4 miles) of hiking and nature trails at Murphy's Landing and the adjacent Memorial Park. The hiking trail is a woods trail from the Memorial Park along the grist mill creek to where the creek joins the Minnesota River. The trail starts at the old prioneer grist mill, crosses the creek, and follows the north bank to the junction with the Minnesota River.

Murphy's Landing Nature Trail is a self-guided nature trail. It is in several loops along grist mill creek and the Minnesota River. A section of *Murphy's Landing Booklet* entitled "A Guide to the Nature Trail" explains many of the natural and historical features one may see along the trail.

For further information write or call:

Murphy's Landing, Box 275
Shakopee, MN 55379
(612) 445-6900

Patrick Eagan Municipal Park

Trail Use: Hiking, Cross-country Skiing
Fee: None

Patrick Eagan Municipal Park is on Dakota County Road 43 (Lexington Avenue) about 5.6 kilometers (3.5 miles) south of Mendota Heights. The park entrance is marked with a sign. A driveway to the park passes a private residence. At the end of the driveway there is parking space, picnic tables, and toilets.

Patrick Eagan Municipal Park is in a wooded valley around 6.8 hectare (17 acre) Lake McCarthy. The forest is mixed hardwoods with some planted conifers. The woods and water make this a beautiful setting. Nestled in a snug little valley, Patrick Eagan Municipal Park seems to be in a world of its own.

TRAIL

The loop trail around Lake McCarthy is 3.2 kilometers (2 miles). Because it was built as a cross-country ski trail, it is wide and well marked. The gentle hills surrounding Lake McCarthy give this ski trail a novice-to-intermediate rating. Although most of the trail is in deep woods, there are open grassy spaces. Along the trail there are rest stops that have benches and fireplaces.

Patrick Eagan Municipal Park is a wildlife Shangri-La that is home base to many birds and mammals.

The trail is well marked and easy to walk. It would be a good trail for a family that is just starting to hike in the wild woods.

For further information write or call:

Park Office
City Hall
Eagan, MN 55122
(612) 454-7802

Phalen Park

Trail Use: Hiking
Fee: None

Phalen Park is a 200 hectare (494 acres) golf course and park located at Burnquist and West Shore Drive. For the visiting public there is a picnic area, and swimming and boating facilities on 78 hectare (193 acres) Lake Phalen.

Phalen Park is named after Edward Phalen who had a claim on Phalen Creek Falls in the years between 1840 and 1844.

TRAIL

The Phalen Park trail is a 4.8 kilometer (3 miles) double parallel set of asphalt paths around the hilly shores of Lake Phalen. One path is for pedestrians and the other is for bicyclists.

Like most of the lakes in Metroland, Phalen Lake attracts waterfowl and other birds.

For further information write or call:

Superintendent of Parks and Recreation
557 City Hall
St. Paul, MN 55102 (612) 298-4126

Ramblin' Rum Campground

Trail Use: Hiking
Fee: User fee for camping, picnicking

Ramblin' Rum Campground is on Anoka County Road 19, about 22 kilometers (14 miles) north of the city of Anoka. This 45 hectare (111 acre) private recreational development is named after the historic Rum River. There are over 300 campsites here which will accommodate everything from backpacking tents to mobile homes.

The lodge has a store and a lounge. Nearby there is a swimming pool and a wading pool. Behind the lodge is a large spring-fed pond. Some of the campsites face this pond. For use on the Rum River, there are both rental canoes and inner tubes. The Rum River is noted for excellent fishing for small mouth bass, walleyes, northern pike, and pan fish.

For daytime visitors, Ramblin' Rum Campground has several large picnic areas that may be reserved for group outings.

TRAILS

At the present time Ramblin' Rum does not have designated hiking or nature trails, but there are many kilometers of informal trails through the forested and prairie hills.

For further information write or call:

Ramblin' Rum Campground
22022 Lake George Blvd. N.W.
Anoka, MN 55303
(612) 753-2211

Ritter Farm Park

Trail Use: Hiking, Cross-country Skiing
Fee: None

This Lakeville Municipal park is west of Interstate 35 on 195th Street.

The park's rolling hills were once crop and pasture lands. While there are some farm woodlots and orchards throughout the park, most of the woods are in the southwest corner.

TRAILS

There are 10.5 kilometers (6.5 miles) of trail in four loops. The loops range from .4 kilometers (.25 miles) to 5 kilometers (3 miles) in length. As ski trails they are rated from intermediate to advanced. The trails start at the parking lot where there are picnic tables and restrooms. A large stationary map shows the trail system. The Ritter Farm Park cross-country ski trail system is made up of old farm roads and new trails. The old farm roads and the ski trails in the wooded areas are easy to follow. The ski trails through the open fields are not marked well enough to be useful for off-season hiking. In time, normal use will take care of this problem. Until then enjoy the wide spacious hills.

For further information write or call:

Parks and Recreation Department
City Hall
Lakeville, MN 55044
(612) 469-5354

Robert E. Ney Memorial Park Reserve

Trail Use: Hiking, Cross-country Skiing
Fee: None

Robert E. Ney Memorial Park Reserve is part of the Wright County Parks Department. It is 3 kilometers (1.9 miles) north of the town of Maple Lake. Turn east off paved County Road 6 and onto a gravel road. The road goes by several residences before coming to a Y intersection next to 94 hectare (232 acres) Mary Lake. Turn to the left. It is a short distance from the junction to the parking lot on the left side of the road.

At the parking lot there is a small picnic area. On a low hill there are several small storage buildings and a brick chapel that is dedicated to the memory of Robert E. Ney.

Robert E. Ney Park Reserve is in a 175 hectare (430 acres) area of forested hills and wetlands. Near the center of park reserve is a 10 hectare (25 acres) pond that drains north through Silver Creek. The forest is thick and tangled and is similar to the northern Minnesota hardwood forests.

TRAILS

At the time I visited Robert E. Ney Memorial Park Reserve there was only one short trail. It started near the chapel and went along the edge of a marsh before coming to an abrupt end in thick brush. Wood duck houses and ruffed grouse were seen on this trail.

When the planned trail system is completed, there will be 9.6 kilometers (6 miles) of trails in this park reserve.

For further information write or call:

Wright County Parks Department
Public Works Building
RFD 1, Box 97-B
Buffalo, MN 55313
(612) 339-6881 Ext. 182

South Washington County Park

Trail Use: Hiking, Cross-country Skiing
Fee: None

This 485 hectare (1200 acres) Washington County Park is in Cottage Grove on the Point Douglas Drive. It is north of U. S. Highways 10-61 which are together at this point. From County Road 19 take the frontage road east to the park entrance. The main park road turns to the right and leads to a picnic area beside a 10 hectare (25 acres) pond.

South Washington County Park is in a range of densely forested moraine hills. Through the center of the park is a deep ravine.

TRAILS

South Washington County Park's trail system is made up of six connected loop trails with a total length of 9.6 kilometers (6 miles). The trails start at the picnic area where a bulletin board with a large stationary map shows the trails.

The trails are used for hiking and cross-country skiing. Some of the trails in the central part of the park are very steep and are rated as advanced ski trails. There are a number of high overlooks in the park that will give the hiker outstanding views of the surrounding countryside. The combination of deciduous and red cedar forest cover makes this park a beautiful place to hike, especially in the fall after the leaves have started to change color.

For further information write or call:

Parks Department
Washington County Courthouse
14900-61st Street N
Stillwater, MN 55082
(612) 439-6058

Check with the Parks Department for maps and other material.

Springbrook Nature Center

Trail Use: Hiking
Fee: None

Springbrook Nature Center is on Anoka County Road 132, west of Minnesota Highway 47 (University Avenue) in Fridley. The parking lot is next to the Center. The Nature Center has a full program of outdoor education. For those who are interested in these programs, it is well to inquire in advance of a planned visit.

TRAILS

Springbrook Nature Center has 4.8 kilometers (3 miles) of nature trails in its 50 hectares (125 acres). The trails start at the parking lot and fan out in a network covering the Center's natural areas. These include forest, prairies, wetlands, creeks, and ponds. The trails even cross marshes by way of boardwalks. Because the Center has several different habitats, it is a good place to look for wildlife. A favorite viewing place is the beaver pond. Many species of wildlife can be seen along the marshy shoreline and open water.

For further information write or call:

Fridley Parks and Recreation Department
6431 University Avenue
Fridley, Minnesota 55432
(612) 560-3450

Maps and trail guides are available from the Parks and Recreation Department.

Stanley Eddy Memorial Park Reserve

Trail Use: Hiking
Fee: None

This developing park is west of Wright County Road 2 about 10 kilometers (6 miles) south of the town of South Haven. South Haven is on Minnesota Highway 55, about 16 kilometers (10 miles) northwest of Maple Plain. Plans call for a parking lot with picnic facilities and a primitive or rustic campground.

Like many of the outdoor recreational areas in Metroland, the topography of Stanley Eddy Memorial Park Reserve is rolling hills covered by deep deciduous forest. Through the wooded hills fast moving strams have cut deep ravines.

This park is being developed as a wild natural area, a place to observe wildlife in their own habitat.

TRAILS

When the park is completed in late 1978, there will be more than 12 kilometers (7.5 miles) of hiking trails.

For further information write or call:

Public Works Building
Wright County Parks Department
RFD 1, Box 97-B
Buffalo, MN 55313
(612) 339-6881 Ext. 182

Tierney's Woods

Trail Use: Hiking, Cross-country Skiing
Fee: None

This undeveloped tract of woods is .4 kilometer (.25 mile) south of Interstate 494 on County Road 18 (Town Line Avenue). Tierney's Woods is a deciduous forest where dominant trees are oak and elm.

TRAILS

At the present time there are no designated hiking trails in Tierney's Woods; however, there are many kilometers of informal trails which are very popular with hikers, cross-country skiers, and bird watchers.

The Bloomington Parks Department is now considering a marked trail system for Tierney's Woods. Also, in the future, there may be connecting trails between the "Woods" and some of the other Bloomington parks. When these trails are completed, it may be possible to hike and ski on trails across town to any of the Bloomington parks.

For further information write or call:

Bloomington Parks and Recreation Department
2215 Old Shakopee Road
Bloomington, MN 55420
(612) 881-5811 Ext. 230

William O'Brien State Park

Trail Use: Hiking, Cross-country Skiing
Fee: Vehicle entrance stamp

William O'Brien State Park is on Minnesota Highway 95 about 25 kilometers (16 miles) north of Stillwater. It is one of several Minnesota and Wisconsin state parks that are located on the historic Saint Croix River.

The 538 hectare (1,330 acres) William O'Brien State Park could be called a campers' park. There are four campgrounds within the boundaries of the park. Two are semi-modern campgrounds with a total of 125 campsites. For organized camping groups such as Scout units and school classes, there is a rustic pioneer group campground with space for 50 campers. Canoeists who paddle the Saint Croix River may camp overnight at a rustic canoe campground. This campground has space for 50 campers.

Because this section of the Saint Croix River is part of the National Wild and Scenic River System, it is now under the management of the National Park Service. The Park Service maintains canoe launching points and campgrounds along the river. Canoe rental and shuttle service are available from park concessionaires.

A modern picnic area with 125 sites is in the woods adjacent to the river. The park's nature center is in the picnic area from which the naturalists conduct an informative interpretative program during the regular visitor season.

HISTORY

During the waning decades of the last ice age, melt water filled the Lake Superior basin. Geologists have named this body of water Glacial Lake Duluth. It was twice as deep as the present Lake Superior and covered a much larger area. For a time the normal outlet to the east was blocked by ice sheets. This resulted in drainage to the south through the valleys of the Brule and Saint Croix Rivers. The tremendous flow of Glacial Lake Duluth water through the Saint Croix River vally cut a wide and deep vale into the rock structure and created a valley of unusual beauty.

HUMAN HISTORY

The now peaceful Saint Croix River valley was once a bloody battleground in the 1730's during a war between the Dakota and the Ojibway Indians. For the Indians the river was an important link in the water route between the Great Lakes and the Mississippi River. After their victory, the Ojibway Indians named the river Man-onin-ikee-ski which means Rice-Bird River. This could be in reference to the river's abundance of wild rice and waterfowl.

With the end of the conflict, fur traders of several nations moved into this valley. It is thought the river was named after a French trader named Sainte-Croix who had a post in the area. In less than one hundred years the fur trader was replaced by the logger and then by the farmer. Now recreation is the chief economic activity of the Saint Croix River valley.

In 1945 the family of pioneer lumberman William O'Brien donated land to the state park system as a memorial to himself. Later the Greenburg family donated Greenburg Island as a memorial to its family members.

VEGETATION

William O'Brien State Park has been both logged and farmed. It is now a patchwork of wooded and open land. The open areas are former cropland and pastures. The result of this mixture of vegetation is an edge between woods and grassland that provides many species of wildlife with better living conditions.

TRAILS

William O'Brien State Park has 22 kilometers (14 miles) of trails that are open to hiking and cross-country skiing. Motorized vehicles are not permitted on these trails.

SAINT CROIX RIVER TRAIL

The Saint Croix River Trail is a 1.6 kilometer (1 mile) loop trail. It starts near the picnic area and loops around the east shore of Alice Like before crossing the main park road to the banks of the Saint Croix River. On the way back to the starting point the trail passes the lower semi-modern campground and the picnic area. Because this trail is through a river bottom forest, you can see the effects of the annual spring floods.

GREENBURG ISLAND TRAIL

Greenburg Island Trail is a 2.4 kilometer (1.5 mile) loop trail around the shores of Greenburg Island. Greenburg Island is across a river channel from the picnic area. In the past there was a foot bridge to the island. However, at the time of my last visit, the bridge had been washed out. It it is not replaced, you will need a boat to get to the Greenburg Island Trail. Like the Saint Croix River Trail, the Greenburg Island Trail is a bottomland forest trail. On the way around the island, the trail passes several small ponds. These are good places from which to observe wildlife.

CROSS-COUNTRY SKI TRAILS

The cross-country ski trails are a system of looped trails through the west side of the park. The total length is about 18.4 kilometers (11.5 miles). The trails start at a parking lot west of the contact station. The parking lot is marked with a sign. From there the trail heads out into the rolling hills in a counter-clockwise direction. Between the forest and grass-covered hills are wide, flat areas of cattail marsh. The main loop is around the edge of marshland and most of it is level. The side loops go up and around some very hilly places. While most of the loops are rated as beginner or intermediate ski trails, some of the steeper loops are rated as advanced. The higher hills offer scenic views of the park and the surrounding countryside.

For further information write or call:

Park Manager
William O'Brien State Park
16821 O'Brien Trail, North
Marine, MN 55047
(612) 433-2421

Wood Lake Nature Center

Trail Use: Hiking, Cross-country skiing
Fee: None

This 60 hectare (148 acres) environmental educational facility is in Richfield. It is close to being in the heart of the Metropolitan area.

The Center is named after, and surrounds, 67 hectare (165 acres) Wood Lake, an open water alkaline marsh. Marshes such as this furnish habitat for many species of wildlife as well as rest stops for migratory birds.

The Nature Center has two parking lots. The larger one which will accommodate buses is at 735 Lake Drive. The smaller parking lot is at Lyndale and 68th Street.

At the Interpretative Center there is an office where visitors should stop for maps and other information. This is also the place to register for guided tours. You may learn much on these tours.

The Center's Museum of Natural History has many different displays of native plants and animals. Open cases have nature items that can be handled for close examination. In the adjoining auditorium the Center's staff conducts nature classes and shows films. There is also a workroom and laboratory.

The Wood Lake Nature Center offers a variety of nature-related learning programs throughout the year. These programs are structured for a wide range of age groups. There are also special programs to meet the needs of the handicapped.

The picnic area has a man-made spring and a shelter with restrooms and water. For children there is a play structure named Fort Apache.

TRAILS

Wood Lake Nature Center has 4.8 kilometers (3 miles) of trails. The trail system is made up of a trail around Wood Lake and several side trails. These side trails lead to observation points overlooking Wood Lake and to various wildlife habitats.

In the winter the trails are groomed for cross-country skiing and are rated as beginner trails.

For further information write or call:

Wood Lake Nature Center
735 Lake Shore Drive
Richfield, MN 55435
(612) 861-4507

University of Minnesota Landscape Arboretum

Trail Use: Hiking, Cross-country Skiing, Snowshoeing
Fee: Parking (Free to Members)

The Arboretum is on Minnesota Highway 5 about 5.6 kilometers (3.5 miles) west of Chanhassen. The entrance to the 227 hectare (560 acres) Arboretum is marked with a sign on the highway. Beyond the gate there is a large parking lot to the left of the main building. If one turns to the right of the main building, it is a short drive to the Arboretum picnic area. The main building acts as a visitor center where there are maps and other material available to the public. There is usually a staff member in the building who is able to answer questions about the Arboretum.

The Arboretum has over 4,000 species of plants. Besides Minnesota plants there are many house and garden plants.

The purpose of the University of Minnesota Landscape Arboretum is to evaluate and develop landscape materials. In doing so, it provides valuable information for those who work with plants.

TRAILS AND ROADS

The Arboretum has a network of intertwined vehicle roads and foot paths. There are 4.8 (3 miles) of asphalt roads and 9.6 kilometes (6 miles) of surface nature trails. There are a number of parking places along the roads. The roads make the nature trails more accessible.

The Arboretum has three nature trails named Wood Duck, Meadowlark, and Green Heron. Each trail is made up of several loops and has a total length of about 3.2 kilometers (2 miles). Along the nature trails are forests, prairies, marshes, and ponds. Much of the Arboretum is wetland and there are long boardwalks over places that are soggy. Some of the boardwalks extend out over ponds where the visitor may observe wildlife. Many varieties of aquatic vegetation can be observed.

Along the roads and trails, plant specimens are marked with names and other information. One will learn much while walking the Arboretum roads and nature trails.

In addition to the nature trails there are many kilometers of recreational trails used for cross-country skiing and snowshoeing. Some of the trails are through lowlands and may be too wet to hike. Check with the Arboretum staff as to the condition of the trails.

For further information write or call:

University of Minnesota Landscape Arboretum
Route 1, Box 132-1
Chaska, MN 55318
(612) 443-2460

The Arboretum has maps that show the roads and trails.

Notes

Notes

Notes

Notes

Suggested Reading

The Magic of Walking by Aaron Sussman and Ruth Goode, Simon and Schuster.

Creative Walking for Physical Fitness by Harry J. Johnson, M.D., Grosset and Dunlap.

Audubon Society Field Guide to North American Birds, Eastern Region by John Bull and John Farrand, Alfred A. Knopf.

Northlands Wild Flowers, A Guide to the Minnesota Region by John Moyle and Evelyn W. Moyle, University of Minnesota Press.

Minnesota's Rocks and Waters by George M. Schwartz and George A. Thiel, University of Minnesota Press.

The Mammals of Minnesota by Harvey L. Gunderson and James R. Beer, University of Minnesota Press.

A Field Guide to Trees and Shrubs by George Petrides, Houghton, Mifflin

The Outdoor Eye, A Sportsman's Guide by Charles Elliott, Outdoor Life, Funk and Wagnalls.

Grazing, The Minnesota Wild Eater's Food Book by Mike Link, Voyageur Press.

The Streams and Rivers of Minnesota by Thomas F. Waters, University of Minnesota Press.